Stop Fixing, Start Leading!®

Engaging America's Workforce

Jack Needham

Eloquent Books
New York, New York

Eloquent Books
An imprint of AEG Publishing Group
845 Third Avenue, 6th Floor – 6016
New York, NY 10022
www.eloquentbooks.com

ISBN: 978-1-60860-034-2   1-60860-034-3

Printed in the United States of America

I would like to dedicate this book to a wise, caring man who has been very supportive throughout my life. He loves me for who I am and never questioned the decisions I made. This man is my father, who is also my coach, friend, guide and, most importantly, my kick-butt advisor.

I would be remiss if I did not dedicate this book as well to all the managers and leaders who have touched my life during my leadership classes and executive coaching. It never ceases to amaze me that leaders who have been in the same leadership practice of command and control for decades can climb out of the river of unconsciousness; they take a deep breath and ask questions that jolt themselves out of their daily routine. With much gratitude I say "Thank you" for your willingness to do something different.

Table of Contents

Acknowledgements

This book would not have been possible without many key people in my life who assisted, encouraged, and sometimes mercilessly prodded me to capture the insights developed as a coach and teacher over the years. I am grateful to the large number of talented, insightful, and generous individuals who helped me to create this book.

I specifically would like to thank my wife Janet, who believed in me even when I did not have the words to describe what I did to assist others in changing their lives. I would also like to thank Steve Hall, who helped take my words and ideas and transform them into this concise yet powerful guide to self-awareness. Thanks to my friends, coaches, and mentors, Tommy Richardson and Rick Valdiserri, for their willingness to be part of the idea-generation sessions that became the outline for this book.

Finally, I would like to deeply thank my clients and students for their feedback and encouragement to write this book. Their affirmation confirms that the practices I share are simple, effective, and life-enhancing.

Introduction

Do you want to become a better manager, a more effective leader in your business? Do you want to create the success you crave, the life you want? Better yet, do you want to help others wake up to those possibilities?

Then stop fixing and start leading.

Traditional business training focuses on fixing productivity, communication, or other issues in the workplace. The problem is that these are *symptoms*, not the underlying cause of the challenges and obstacles you face with your employees. If your car engine developed a knocking sound when you reached a certain speed on the highway, would you simply drive slower? Or keep the windows rolled up so you couldn't hear the sound? No, you or a professional mechanic would uncover the cause of the knocking in the engine so you could eliminate it.

In the same way, a manager who attempts to correct absenteeism or increase a department's sales only through old methods or approaches is applying a temporary fix at best. True leadership involves changing employees' beliefs by helping them gain self-awareness and accountability for their actions.

The main reason that people tend to make poor decisions or careless mistakes is that they don't think their actions through. In terms of awareness they are totally asleep, drifting through the motions of their job without much thought about what they're doing. They are letting what I call "the river of unconsciousness" sweep them along.

Your job as a leader is to wake them up. *Stop Fixing, Start Leading!*® will show you how. Instead of an alarm clock, you will learn to use:

- trust-building exercises

- masterful questions

- verbal imaging

- "sacred listening," that is, engaged and unfiltered listening

- the art of awareness

- the art of choices, and

- the art of practice.

Most managers who are drifting in the river of unconsciousness concentrate on reports, metrics, procedures, and other such systemic repetition. They *manage*, and nothing more. They cannot distinguish between management activities and true leadership. When those with management-only attitudes drift down the river of unconsciousness, swollen egos keep them afloat. Those egos fool the managers into believing that to be a leader, they must be superior. They must direct, order, discipline, tell, and condescend. In their minds "leader" and "manager" are the same things.

However, some people climb out of the river of unconsciousness by taking a deep breath and thinking thoughts and asking questions that jolt themselves out of their daily routine. This is like climbing onto a rock in the river where they can gain a new perspective on everything around them. Those who find the rock become aware of true leadership characteristics such as sacred listening, masterful questioning, and non-threatening language. Their actions provide guidance to their employees and cause shifts in thought that lead to ultimately positive behavior because the employees are able to choose their actions from a higher level of awareness.

Just about anyone with linear capabilities can be a manager if the systems are set to report and repeat. However, only those who come in touch with their own being become self-aware, and shift their own behavior are in a position to build strong leadership qualities.

In my first book, *The Zebra Hunter*, I described how my experiences during the months spent caring for an AIDS patient taught me lessons that have transformed my life. The title comes from the gentle wisdom of the man I was caring for. Every morning he looked out his window in hopes of seeing a zebra. Now, seeing a zebra might have been likely if he lived in Africa or next to a zoo, but he lived in Carmel, Indiana—not exactly known as a home of free-ranging zebras. When I pointed this out, he replied, "True, I haven't seen one yet, but I never stop looking." He taught me much about the power of positive thinking and seeing the possibilities in life and in people.

This book is about seeing the possibilities for greatness in your employees and helping them achieve that greatness. So stop fixing! Start leading!

Chapter 1

Everybody's Perfect

A very old traditional brewery decided to install a new canning line so it could market its beer products in supermarkets. This represented a major change for the little company, and local dignitaries and past employees were invited to witness the first running of the new canning line, which was followed by a buffet and drinks.

After the new line had been successfully switched on, the guests chatted and enjoyed the buffet. In a quiet corner three men discussed trucks and distribution, since one was the present distribution manager and the other two, both retirees, had held the job many years ago. The three men represented more than sixty years of company distribution management.

The present distribution manager confessed that his job was becoming more stressful because company policy required long-distance deliveries to be made on Monday and Tuesday, short-distance deliveries on Fridays, and all other deliveries mid-week. "It's so difficult to schedule things efficiently," he said. "Heaven knows what we'll do with these new cans and the tight demands of the supermarkets."

The other two men nodded in agreement. "It was the same in my day," said the present manager's predecessor. "*It always seemed strange to me that trucks returning early on Mondays and Tuesdays couldn't be used for little local runs, because the local deliveries had to be left until Friday.*"

The oldest man thought hard, struggling to recall the policy's roots many years ago when he worked in the dispatch department. "I remember now," he said. "It was the horses. During the Second World War fuel rationing was introduced. So we mothballed the trucks and went back to using the horses. On Mondays the horses were well-rested after the weekend—hence the long-distance deliveries. By Friday the horses were so tired they could only handle the local drops."

Soon after that, the company changed its delivery policy.—Ack R Chagar

As with the preceding tale, many organizations continue to do what they have always done, even the management of others, because this is the way that it has always been done. Then we wonder why it is that we are not getting different results!

The first thing I want to share with you is that no one needs to be fixed. Everyone is perfect just the way they are. As the brewery delivery story illustrates, they are sometimes just not conscious of why they're doing the same thing over and over and what needs to change.

Is that sales rep not making her quotas? What about the IT guy who can't explain anything in plain English and accidentally crashed the system last week?

Both perfect, just the way they are.

Managers and employers need to realize that employees' behavior stems from their conditioning—a type of learning that instilled and reinforced behavior clues from people and events, usually in their childhoods. They go to work with this conditioning embedded in their subconscious. They might learn something new at work that becomes part of their conditioning, and then they continue to do the same thing over and over again.

This conditioning is not wrong; the employee is fine the way he or she is. The employee just needs to wake up from this conditioning. That waking up is dependent upon the manager asking them the right questions or helping them see things a little differently. It's that simple. We can't be responsible *for* them changing, but we can be responsible *to* help them change.

If we continue to look at the flaws in their behavior, that attention magnifies those flaws, and soon we only focus on what's not working. Let's say the only time someone is approached, whether in relationships or at work, is in regards to something that's not working. Soon those flaws are all we see, and the other person comes to dread our approach because that person expects us to only talk about the flaws. We have *conditioned* them to expect that.

Perception reveals to us that, within our perfection, everybody's flawed. The employees, you and I—we're all flawed. Most times when we're reflecting back to the person what needs to change in him or her, we have the same flaw. We're blinded by what we think is their problem when, in reality, most of the time it is *our* problem too. That's why we are so easily able to see it.

The analogy I would draw is buying a car. Before you buy a car, you look at many different vehicles, makes, and models, but you don't particularly notice them on the road. As soon as you buy a particular model and drive it off the lot—let's say a

Toyota Corolla—your awareness "pops" and you see Toyota Corollas everywhere.

While we see our flaws in others, we can also experience that "awareness pop" with good things too. Usually we manage by reacting to "what was"—last quarter's sales, for example. We need to change our mindset and see the greatness, see the possibilities. We need to see "what is" to awaken our employees.

If you look at "what is" and ask masterful questions, the possibility of that awareness factor getting bigger starts to grow, and that greatness starts to develop within that individual from the very first masterful question.

As I mentioned previously, most of the time, people are stuck in "the river of unconsciousness." As you're flowing down the river with a current that's very strong, you seldom have the chance to take a breath. But from time to time, if somebody asks an insightful question or makes a comment that causes you to think, it's like grabbing onto a rock, standing up on that rock, and being able to take a deep breath. For the first time in months or years, you see everything around you from a different perspective because you are not sucked along and under by the current.

I guarantee that because of human nature, people will jump right back into the river of unconsciousness. The current will carry them further along until another masterful question is asked and they get up on the rock again. They might keep doing that again and again until they actually climb out of the river on their own for a moment or two before jumping back in. At some point they realize they don't have to stay in the current and be unconscious.

Taking things personally can keep us drifting in the river of unconsciousness. Thinking that people are out to get us when they're not can be so real and magnifying that people hang onto that delusion for a day, a week, a month, sometimes their whole lifetime.

The reality: Life's not just about you. The person who spread that rumor about you or forced you off the lucrative account did so because that's all they know—from their conditioning. When you realize they acted that way because they're stuck in their own river of unconsciousness, you can make a shift in your own conditioning. You can realize: "What can I do differently, how can I do things differently, how can I not do what *they* did?" By asking masterful questions, you start to move away from that hurt, that pain, that struggle.

This is not to disparage your emotions, which are very real. Nor should you accept when someone does something bad to you or is harsh to you. But if you can see things differently based on the questions you ask yourself, you can help alleviate the problem. You may choose not to be around that person, place, or condition, but at least you're coming back into your own mind with empowering—not debilitating— thoughts. You become the most powerful source of making powerful choices versus being at the whim of another's action.

I learned the wisdom of not taking things personally when I was growing up in a family of eight children. My dad served in the Air Force, and we traveled around the world. That nomadic lifestyle and such a large family carried a lot of stresses and pressures, but I never got caught up in the drama. Instead I learned to look at each situation and think: What did I learn from this person, place, or condition?

As I grew older, I realized that our perspective comes from our conditioning—that what we consider "reality" is just our conditioning. I realized that conditioning makes us who we are and who the other person is as well. For that reason, becoming angry about someone's comments or actions would be as futile as looking at a gray table and becoming angry because it's gray. The table has no control over its grayness; it is its nature to be gray, and its nature isn't going to change for you, me, or anyone else!

When you take things personally, you shut down the relationship with the other person because of a lack of trust. When a boss approaches an employee, the emotional history of any prior interaction shows up in that moment. If the interactions have been negative, the employee will expect more negativity and the trust will not be there.

How can we approach employees in a way to successfully modify their behavior? Usually problems arise not because of what is said, but because of what we assume. We often assume that the employee knows what to do in a certain situation because *we've* done it. If the employee has never faced that situation before, how could he or she know how to handle it? How can we help the person learn and see what needs to be done?

We lead by asking masterful questions. As managers and leaders, we are accountable to ask the questions that are currently not being asked.

Once we start asking the right questions, will the employee "get it"? It depends on their frame of mind. Someone once compared enlightenment, or a willingness to change, to that of a leaf falling from a tree. If people are ready for change, the leaf could hit them in the head with the softness of a feather and they would become enlightened. If they are not ready, the whole tree could fall on them and they would still be clueless.

The first level of all change is self-awareness. When we help people become aware of themselves, they become aware of their body, of their breathing, and of their thoughts. A recent statistic said that 80 to 85 percent of all doctor visits are stress-induced. If people were just aware of their breathing for thirty days, they would have the possibility of calming themselves and lowering their blood pressure and stress level.

Becoming aware of your breathing might seem like a small thing, but it is not. When you concentrate on your breathing, walking, typing, or anything else, you are living in the moment and not worrying about the past or dreaming about the future. The river of unconsciousness ceases to control you. You are self-aware.

Is self-awareness easy to achieve? No. Someone once said that my awareness training is tough work. It's tough because in learning to be conscious of your feelings and expectations—what you want more of, what you want less of—you make a choice on how to live each moment. And while that sounds tough, everything is *already* a choice. Most of us are just not self-aware enough to realize it.

The training you will receive in this book will give you the ability to recognize others' level of awareness. They may have high self-awareness and live in the moment, or they may have low self-awareness and be stuck in the river of unconsciousness. You as a manager must realize that whatever their level of awareness, they are showing up as best they can in the present moment. In the present moment that's who they are.

No one wakes up in the morning and thinks, "Hey, I'm gonna screw up my life today!" Instead, most of us drift along in the river of unconsciousness and make the same mistakes over and over until questions from a masterful teacher—who could be a manager, leader, mentor, coworker, family member, or friend—helps wake us up so we may change.

In changing employees' behavior, it's critical to view and change the deed instead of judging the doer. You need to question the doer about the deed and help him or her see the consequences of how they do the deed. But you don't judge the doer because the deed is not working.

Here's an example: Let's say I write on a balloon why a particular person irritates me. Judging the doer for each wrong deed is like blowing up the balloon a little more each time. Pretty soon when I approach that person, the only thing he or she will see in the encounter is this huge balloon saying "You irritate me." That does not lead to a productive exchange.

You need also to be aware of the grief process involved in change. When you become self-aware, you realize that you are not who you thought you were. Letting go of that self-image is a sort of death. The feelings that you experience mirror the five stages in which people deal with grief and tragedy, as described by Elizabeth Kübler-Ross in her book *On Death and Dying*: Denial, anger, bargaining, depression, and acceptance.

As managers and leaders, we must remember that when we change employees' conditioning, they will grieve for the person they were or the job they used to do before they embrace the change.

Embracing this change is key to employees engaging in their jobs, i.e., being productive and loyal to the company or business. Substantial research indicates that when employees are engaged, productivity, customer satisfaction, service, employee retention, and financial performance rise.

An ongoing Gallup study reported recently that only 29 percent of the U.S. working population is engaged. The study found that 56 percent of U.S. workers are "just putting in time," while 15 percent are unhappy, looking to leave, or spreading discontent among their coworkers or customers. When employees are not engaged, customer satisfaction, financial performance, and the other factors above decline. There is a huge profit loss when employees are not engaged.

In the modern workforce few employees work for the same company for 20 or 30 years. They have choices. If you ask the masterful questions that will help them grow, however, their ability to perform increases exponentially with their awareness, and so does their engagement with their job. Productivity, customer satisfaction, financial performance all increase.

Often, in order to change conditioning, the person needs to change his or her self-talk, the things we tell ourselves. If each of us was a computer, self-talk would be the programming that determines how we operate.

I am a Self-Talk trainer, certified by psychologist Dr. Shad Helmstetter, who wrote the book *What to Say When You Talk to Yourself.* Dr. Helmstetter's book is a primer on how the brain works. Basically, he discovered that the things we tell ourselves create our belief in who we are and what we're capable of. That belief creates the attitude with which we view the world. That attitude creates our feelings, and our feelings create results, namely the actions that show up in the environment.

Do you hear yourself or someone else chant such mantras as: yeah, of course I dropped my toast jelly-side down because I'm always so clumsy, and I didn't send out that birthday card on time because I always forget, and of course I missed the elevator again, and there's that meeting today that I should have prepared better for – stupid, stupid, stupid!

How do you think that person's day is going to go?

Self-talk can serve as a powerful tool in conditioning ourselves. Phrases such as "I have talents, skills, and abilities, and I'm discovering new talents all the time" can control our mindsets and optimize our outlooks. When you listen carefully to your employees' self-talk, clues to their conditioning become obvious.

In training sessions I have participants eliminate negative self talk such as "coulda," "woulda," "shoulda." Since you can't change anything in the past, those words have no meaning. The same is true of "I need to," "I have to," "I want to." Hey, you don't *need* to or *have* to do anything. The real question is: *Will* you do it? What are the questions that help you to take action? What is your commitment to change?

Self-talk clues can tell you that the employee is stuck in the past or that no commitment to change exists. When an employee says, "I'll try to get that project done by Thursday" rather than "I'll get that project done by Thursday," they have no real commitment to action. When you recognize these clues, you can ask the masterful questions that will help the employee take the steps to move forward.

But remember this: When pushing your employees for greater self-awareness, you must be the example you want your employees to see! Mahatma Gandhi said, "Be the change you want to see in the world." If you want your employees to be more engaged, what are *you* doing to be more engaged? Are you committed to creating trust rather than breaking trust? *You* must be what you want to see. Only then can you always invite greatness in others.

In training and workshops I discover what people want to be by what they don't want anymore. What they want is seeking them as much as they are seeking it; you must help them realize their potential by taking away what they don't want or need. Michelangelo said, "I saw the angel in the marble and carved until I set him free." You as the leader must act as the sculptor, carving away what obscures the greatness within those who look to you for guidance.

I had my own Tae Kwon Do school for years. Often a new student came to me and said he wanted to be the next Jet Li or Jackie Chan when he knew nothing about this martial art. I would focus on the part of him that aspired to be Jet Li or Jackie Chan and teach him the skills necessary for his dream. This step-by-step process helped them become what they wanted.

You can help your employees realize their potential. The first step is changing the way you communicate.

KEY POINTS: EVERYBODY'S PERFECT

- Everybody's perfect just the way they are. The problem is their conditioning from past experiences. They drift along making the same mistakes over and over.

- "Reality" is just our conditioning. Instead of reacting to "what was," change employees' conditioning by asking masterful questions that force them to climb out of the river of unconsciousness, think differently, and ultimately display different behaviors.

- You must help an employee change his or her self-talk to change their behavior.

- When pushing your employees for greater self-awareness, be the change you want to see.

Chapter 2

No Assumptions

A group of suppliers was being given a tour of a mental hospital. One of the visitors made some insulting remarks about the patients.

After the tour the visitors were introduced to various members of staff in the cafeteria. The rude visitor chatted with Bill, one of the orderlies.

"Is everyone in here a raving loony?" asked the rude man.

"Only the ones who fail the test," said Bill.

"What test?" asked the man.

"We show them a bathtub full of water, a bucket, a jug, and a glass," said Bill. "We ask them what's the quickest way to empty the tub."

"Oh, it's simple," the visitor said. "The normal ones know it's the bucket, right?"

"No—the normal ones say pull out the plug," said Bill. "Should I check when there's a bed free for you?"

Our judgments about others are the first thing that get in the way of our understanding who they are and how they operate. We have a tendency to assume that the person or persons that work for us are just like us, should know what we are talking about, should know what we are meaning in our conversations with them, and most of all should know what to do before we tell them. Just as the wrong assumption was made in the story, we too must become cognizant of what assumptions we are making of our employees.

I was introduced many years ago to a book called *The Four Agreements*, a bestselling book by Don Miguel Ruiz, which is a powerful exploration of self-talk. The author explains the source of self-limiting beliefs that rob us of joy and create needless suffering in relationship with others. They offer four agreements that we can make with ourselves—seemingly simple agreements that can transform our lives. The four agreements are:

1. **Be impeccable with your word.** Speak with integrity. Say what you mean, mean what you say. Don't beat up people with your words.

2. **Don't take anything personally.** You will remember this from the first chapter. The book points out this as the highest form of arrogance because you think that is about you.

3. **Don't make assumptions.** Another form of arrogance.

4. **Always do your best.** That best may change from day to day, but intention is the key.

The third agreement is the one I wish to explore here. Making assumptions is the biggest problem with managers and leaders today. They assume that if they tell someone what to do, the person will do it. The majority of the time, the assumption is that the person has enough information to do what needs to be done. But depending on the trust level with the manager, the employee may not ask questions because there is no trust. And so things don't get done, and people get angry. They try to "fix" things or "fix" people.

Imagine if the manager was to ask a question, such as "What was your take on what we just said?" Something that simple might help you wake up to the possibility that the employee got it—or didn't. That kind of question invites conversation.

The more curious you are as a manager, the better your working relationship with your employees will be. The curious state will discover what the person knows. Sure, telling someone what to do is simpler, but a weakness lies in the telling. By telling the employee, we're missing opportunities to help that person wake up. By being curious, we have the opportunity to ask the next question that might wake that person up.

We need to question the status quo. By its nature, life is dynamic. People are always concerned or stressed out by change, but the only constant that exists is change. If you don't question the status quo, you don't have access to alternate outcomes. Ask yourself "What didn't I ask that, if I had, that person, place, or condition might be different?"

Don't settle for "I'm the manager, the leader, the owner of the business. This is what needs to be done." Stay curious. Help develop the people to become so capable and have such a high level of trust that when you say, "Do something," there is no thought as to whether it will get done or not.

Developing someone to that level is not easy. We hire people with the capability to get something done, but in that hiring process are we putting them in the position to succeed or fail? I run into this situation again and again, where people are put in management and leadership positions but have no ability to lead. Why?

Many businesses like to promote from within. For example, the dynamic, highest-performing salesperson in an organization might be promoted to sales manager. But what if he or she has no ability to lead? Their inability to lead might start destroying the sales force.

If something in your workplace is not working, can you see beyond what is not working? Many times what is not working is just that—it is not working! The illusion is that what's not working is more prevalent than what the organization needs to work, and may even be true! However, if we focus on the problem, that will only get bigger. If we truly want things to change, we must ask ourselves: How can we help that person on what we want to create together? How can we partner together to help them see beyond "what-ifs"?

As I explained in the last chapter, it is critical to view the deed and address what's not working, rather than judging the doer. You should look at the deed and realize it is what it is. It's not going to change because it's already done. You instead question the doer, "What was the thinking behind what you did? What worked and what didn't because of that?" All of a sudden this masterful questioning allows the person to see things differently, rather than feeling judged because of what they did.

If you help them see the consequences of their actions—"What's the outcome if you do that again?"— they start to see the image in their mind of the possibility of not getting the sale or improving their communications with a coworker. They climb out of the river of unconsciousness for an instant and see the image of what's not working.

If they see that image, they have the potential to realize, "Hey, that's not what I want." If it's not what they want, your questions about what they *do* want can create a different image in their minds and provide the outcome you want.

Let me explain how we as human beings think in images. If I say "garbage can," your mind doesn't see "g-a-r-b-a-g-e-c-a-n." No, you picture a garbage can, probably round, maybe black or silver, either with the lid clamped down tight on its smelly, messy contents or showing that garbage to the world.

Every time you or I ask a really good question, the brain of the person hearing the question creates an image. If that image is only of what's not working, that's all that person will see, and they won't change their behavior no matter how hard we want them to. Their lack of commitment is directly correlated to the strength of the image they have in their minds.

Masterful questions allow that person to see things differently—literally, from an image point of view. Ask enough masterful questions, and the image is so powerful that the person has the experience of change in the mind. Their commitment to change becomes more real versus just a conversation of "Do this, do that."

In the questioning of the doer, you have to be observant of the body. Often we listen, but a lot of things happen with non-words. It goes back to "coulda, woulda, shoulda." They're non-words since the events they refer to are in the past and the speaker has no possibility of changing them—or, for that matter, possesses no real intent to change them. They might say, "Sometimes I do that." "Sometimes" is a relative term.

By listening to the non-words and the words that are always relative, you can have the possibility of seeing and addressing some weaknesses. Rather than just staying stuck in what's not working, you can ask masterful questions, learn what they're really saying and solidify the image of where they want to go.

For example, let's say a manager tells me he would like to see his salespeople make 20 percent more sales.

I would say, "When was the last time you had a 20 percent or more increase in sales?"

"Well … never."

"What was the highest increase in sales you've had?"

"Uh … nine percent."

"OK. Let's be successful at what we've already done and call that success. Let's talk about what happened to create that nine percent increase. What were some specific behaviors you instilled in your sales force at that point in time to help them realize that nine percent increase? Have them practice that once again to achieve what they've already accomplished. Then let's talk about some new practices to increase sales further. What's one additional thing we could do to increase the sales by two percent?"

"OK."

Through these questions I would help him uncover and discover what has already worked and solidify the image of those successful practices in his mind. Usually when someone comes to me with a problem, he or she has usually conquered that issue in the past. But after a time, the person jumped back into the river of unconsciousness and forgot what used to work. You go in incremental stages because whatever you practice shows up.

Let's talk for a moment about what we practice shows up in our life. If you practice anger in life, it shows up in every relationship. It shows up in the car if you're driving on the highway and someone pulls in front of you. It shows up as you kick the dog. If you practice great communication skills, that's what shows up as well. If you practice becoming a martial artist, then that's what shows up.

What are *you* practicing? What are your salespeople practicing? Because whatever they practice, shows up. If they practice being knowledgeable and courteous, that's what shows up. If they practice being disorganized and surly, chaos and anger show up. It's as simple as that. It's just not easy to change. If they practice great closing skills or call reluctance, it shows up!

Only seven percent of our ability to communicate is comprised of the words we use. Yet we spend 98 percent of our time communicating with words. How much are we, as managers and leaders, missing if we don't pay attention to body and tone when we talk to our employees? It's huge.

Studies show that 55 percent of communication is with the body. In fact, researchers said, sometimes the body is so loud that the other person can't hear what is said. If you ask your spouse what's wrong and they say "Nothing" but their arms are folded, there's obviously something wrong.

That goes to the next piece, which is voice tone. The voice is 38 percent of your ability to communicate in every relationship we have.

If the body and tone are off, you know that there's something that needs to be uncovered. It's an obvious sign that the other person is not saying something or doesn't trust you.

Part of building trust is not having the drama show up in the conversations you have. If you come to a person who practices anger, judgment, resentment, that's what shows up in the conversation—and how much trust do you think might appear? If you show up just curious and not judgmental, looking at the facts, looking at the deed and not the doer, you have a possibility of opening up something that was not discussed before, that's always been hidden.

It's all because you're bringing the curiosity, not the drama. And the curiosity is there to help that person develop and change. If you make it about them, about their agenda, then all of a sudden the trust comes up. The benefit: the higher the trust, the bigger the commitment to change.

It's really critical to always speak your truth. But understand that it's *your* truth, based on what you've experienced from birth until now. And your truth is different from their truth. To see what their truth is, help them see what worked for them.

The best analogy is that a lot of people have been conditioned throughout their life to give 55 to 60 percent of what they're capable of giving. With the ability to question that status quo that conditioning will no longer work, depending on who they are and based on what has happened to them up until now. Whatever business you're in, whether you're working the fast-food window at McDonald's, assembling engines for airplanes, or whatever, you're preparing yourself for whatever is next.

In that preparation, what outcomes do you want? Do you just want to work and continue to be here, or do you want to look at the possibility of going to college or whatever it may be? That possibility exists in helping a person see his or her truth. If you help them seek his or her truth, trust goes up incredibly.

Being their mirror is about helping them see what they're saying by helping them view what they're doing. "What worked in this sales call? What didn't work? What outcomes would you like to see in the next call? To achieve that, what needs to change?"

Employees may not be aware of what they did in a certain situation until you show them. Most people are not conscious of some of the counterproductive things they say or do.

By being their mirror and reflecting their image back to them, you allow them to see the consequences of their actions. That helps clarify for the employees. They can learn to say to themselves, "That outcome is not what I want" or "What *do* I want to happen in this situation?" "I can no longer say I did this because of my parents" or "I can't say I didn't close the deal solely because of the client's past history with our company." They become aware there are consequences for choosing what they've always done.

Seeing the consequences brings accountability to your actions. When you are awake, you realize that everything is a choice and you can no longer blame anyone else for the decisions you have made. You have 100 percent responsibility for everything that goes on in your life—even the conditioning that you now have.

A friend of mine is a good person, but in his early fifties he still blames his childhood for the problems and challenges of his life. Recently he called me because he had gotten fired from his latest job. I said, "You gotta wake up. You can't do this anymore. You can't blame people, places, or conditions for your problems. You're just getting the same thing over and over again, but you expect a different result. That's called insanity." He needs to accept responsibility for his life and he now does because of challenging his status quo!

One of the greatest mind shifts that managers and leaders can make is that we can only coach to *"what is,"* not *"what if."* Any time I engage in leadership coaching, people bring in scenarios and then start to question, "But what if we did this? What if we did that?" I say, "It doesn't matter because it hasn't happened. The only thing you can do is practice the simplicity of asking questions now, right here in the present moment. That's when you're going to master the skill of asking questions."

Staying with "what ifs" will always keep you stuck because you're not changing your internal personal behaviors. Practice the skills that will help you change the present moment, which will lead to the next moment, and the next. When you show up in those moments, you have a skill of asking masterful questions that help people wake up and do things differently. If you always practice the "what if," by contrast, you won't practice the questioning skill—you'll only practice the "what if."

When I am present, I can be with everything that the person is asking. Usually their truth is in the last few words of the last sentence they say. That's where I ask the next question, so it will always be in context to where they are in the conversation.

So if the client said, "I'm satisfied with your X2000 because of its durability," the salesperson might say, "I hear you saying you like the X2000 because it's durable. Are you aware that the X2001 is built and programmed to the same exacting standards, but has these additional features that would be extremely useful for your business?"

It's not wrong to practice the "what if" scenario in an analytical sense regarding decision-making for the future. But regardless of how much you want things to change, nothing can change except in the right here and now.

KEY POINTS: NO ASSUMPTIONS

- Don't make assumptions. Instead, ask a question that might help wake you to the understanding of whether or not the employee understood you.

- Because human beings think in images, use questions to create powerful images in conversation to help the employee's commitment to change become real.

- Whatever you practice in life shows up. For the best results with employees, practice curiosity and a genuine interest in them.

- When you help someone seek his or her truth, their level of trust in you goes up incredibly.

- While asking "what if" can be beneficial in planning for the future, true change can only occur in the here and now.

Chapter 3

Transform Fear into Trust

The Great Zumbrati successfully completed a tightrope walk over Niagara Falls, made even more dangerous by a high wind and driving rain. When Zumbrati finally reached solid ground again, he was met by one of his biggest fans. The fan urged him to make a return trip, this time pushing a wheelbarrow, which the man had thoughtfully brought along.

Given the terrible conditions, the Great Zumbrati was understandably reluctant to attempt the feat. But his fan pressed him. "You can do it," he urged. "I know you can."

"You really believe I can do it?" asked Zumbrati.

"Yes, definitely!" gushed the fan. "You can do it."

"Okay," said Zumbrati. "Get in the wheelbarrow."

What is the level of trust that you have with your employees? Is what you are saying or doing building or destroying the trust?

Trust is the essential ingredient for any successful organization. Stephen M.R. Covey's book *The Speed of Trust: The One Thing That Changes*

Everything talks about how bureaucratic checks and balances are often used in the workplace in lieu of actual trust and how trust functions in every relationship and transaction, whether personally or professionally.

Managers and leaders need to look at what trust is: what is trust to them and what is it to others. Webster's defines trust as "assured reliance on the character, ability, strength, or truth of someone or something." To me, trust is authenticity combined with vulnerability. When you rely on the other person because of those qualities, it makes you vulnerable to an outside source of influence.

What happens when someone interacts with you and there is trust or no trust? What causes trust to be created? Where does it start? How do I walk into an interaction with a customer or employee and consciously start creating trust? What actions and behaviors am I displaying that display lack of trust? What needs to change in me, the words I use or behaviors I exhibit, for the possibility of trust to take place?

In my experience it comes down to "How much do I trust myself?" The more I trust myself, the more I trust others. I trust my thoughts, the words I say, the actions I take. When you show up as the message you want people to see, they know that you're a person of integrity and credibility. They know that there's something there that they want for themselves. Some might say trust is not tangible, but it's very tangible. How can you approach someone in an open manner that invites trust?

When I have dealings with someone who is untrustworthy, I tell myself, "That person is where they are in life and I'm just not going to play with that person." Is it discernment, judgment, or lack of trust? I trust others to the degree that I trust myself. The more you trust yourself, the more you come to trust your intuition. You trust decisions that you make that are best for everybody concerned in the present moment.

Look at your own experience and remember someone you trust highly. If you remember the words they've used interacting with you, the words were conducive to your growth and supportive of you, but were seldom non-judgmental. The intention was to help you grow, to be conscious of your decisions, and to make those decisions that would make your life better. Because that intention is positive, the relationship you have is an unbreakable bond.

What words are you using when you approach others? What is your intention? Is your intention to focus on what's not working, or is it to help others grow and see things differently? Look at the words they use, the intention behind those words and the relationship you have. That's what they call the trust level.

Let's say you're shopping for a new laptop. At one store you find a model you like, and the salesperson's pitch about the fabulous warranty on this model convinces you to buy it. Six months later you begin having problems with the screen. "Thank goodness my warranty covers that," you think, and take the laptop back to the store. A customer service representative tells you that fixing the screen will cost $250 and your warranty does not cover it. You feel burned by the original salesperson. Your perceptions of that salesperson and store will be colored by that experience and you will feel a lack of trust.

This goes back to my original statement about the importance of not taking things personally. Feeling that the original salesperson "pulled one over" on you does not allow us to discover who that person was, why he made those comments, and what things you should have done differently to have a different experience. That different experience is the critical part of growing. My choice would be to not have a relationship with that person!

Again, the lack of trust leaves you vulnerable to taking things personally. In the case of the computer store salesman, you probably think, "This guy screwed me." In reality, that guy probably "screws" everyone.

This brings us to the subject of trust in relationships versus conditions. Conditions will always be what they are. Building trust between two individuals is crucial to transmute those conditions. If we focus on the conditions only, there will be no trust and nothing will change. The transformation must take place in the relationship before the conditions will change.

I was doing a team-selling concepts seminar for a large organization in Chicago. One manager asked, "Isn't the environment going to impact your attitude?" I said, "Absolutely—but it cannot control it. That's your choice."

The Seven Habits of Highly Successful People by Stephen R. Covey (Stephen M.R.'s dad) contains a diagram showing how we're constantly bombarded with things that concern us. The center reflects our amount of influence. Just outside the center is a circle representing our immediate consciousness—what concerns us on a personal level every day. Outside that circle is another, bigger circle representing concerns out in the world—the war in Iraq, oil issues, global warming, and so on.

How much control do we have over that second, outermost circle of concern? Very little. We mainly ignore it because we feel we can't do anything to change it. But the smaller inner circle of concern always impacts our ability to make decisions.

According to Covey, the only way you can make an impact on your concerns is with influence. The only way you can influence is in what you say and do. What you say and do helps create trust, and that core of influence starts to get bigger and the concerns start to become less. The bigger your core of influence, the less you have to do because you're no longer trying to fix things. You have influenced everyone to think independently, ask masterful questions, and consider different perspectives. You have created an environment of trust.

I was sitting by a lake in Brown County, Indiana. There was no wind, and the lake was crystal-clear, like glass. When I looked into the water, I could see the reflection of the trees on the other bank and the sky and clouds above. I could not tell the difference between what was real and what was the reflection. Then I threw a pebble into the water, causing ripples to go out and out, into infinity. The pebble erupted the clarity, erupted the experience.

Reflecting on what needs to change in you is like throwing that pebble. Only then can you distinguish between reality and illusion and become clear about what needs to be done to establish trust. You must ask yourself: "What am I learning about myself from this person, place, or condition? What do I need to do differently?"

When you become curious about another person, he or she can see that you're sincere about helping him or her grow, that you are no longer interested in accusing him or her of screwing up intentionally, in condemning behavior. That leads the other person to trust you, and that trust frees the person up for a behavior shift.

What are the behaviors that cause lack of trust? Micro-managing shows that you do not trust someone else to do something right; you are constantly looking over his or her shoulder, expecting a screw-up at any moment. You're always double-checking their work because you don't trust their ability. It is easier and takes less time to "fix" a work issue by telling someone what to do than helping them become the change you want to see.

It's very hard for someone who is not aware to change. The resistance to change comes from not being aware. Think about times when someone has tried to force you to do anything. You became resistant, right?

But what if that manager stopped micro-managing and instead saw each employee as a person? What if that manager saw the potential in each employee—saw what he or she is and what they can do versus the limited conditions that manager currently sees?

Condemning is the easiest thing to do because it's pure judgment. What masterful question would I ask instead of condemning? That question alone has the possibility of helping that employee see something different because it's in question form. It's not a statement only. The statements only and observations of judgment that we have destroy trust.

Ultimately you, as a manager and leader, have to ask yourself: "What about me? What am I doing to condition this person, place, or thing? What's my part in this?" Unfortunately when a leader is a micro-manager, they condition their employees to behave a certain way, and the employees become compliant. They comply with the conditions—and it's still not good enough for the micro-manager.

In my experience, micro-managing stems from the manager's fear of what will and won't get done. They impose that fear on the people who work for them, and therefore there is no trust.

Think about who you trust highly. With them there is no thought about what you would say and do. You ask them to do something; they're going to do it. It doesn't mean that you never double-check their work; it just means that you help them understand that they're accountable. You think that trust stems from that individual's personality. While it does, it also stems from the conditioning of that individual.

In the micro-managing example, I suspect the leader would have to admit to themselves that they don't have a lot of trust anywhere.

Mastery of trust begins with taking a hard look at yourself and asking, "What am I fearful of?" It's OK to be fearful in some situations. It keeps you from getting hit by a car in the street; it keeps you from doing stupid things. But that fearfulness can get in the way of building trust. How much is that fear getting in the way of you trusting yourself? When you show up fully trusting in situations at work, you have a better possibility of fully trusting someone else.

You handle that fearfulness by being aware, by taking a breath, and asking yourself: "Is it real? Is it justified?" Mark Twain once said, "There has been much tragedy in my life; at least half of it actually happened." That speaks to our unfounded fears. How many of us waste our time on unnecessary worrying about something, and it never happens? Yet what was your image during that time of worrying? What was your self-talk, your relationships, like in those conditions?

Over the years I have wanted to trust some people and not others. I have discovered through my life experience that if I trust myself implicitly, I have a much bigger capacity for trusting others. Some individuals *are* untrustworthy. I can still trust my interactions with them, however, because of my ability to discern their truthfulness and to decide whether I want to play with them.

It comes back to: I make better decisions and have better relationships in every situation—coaching, teaching, it doesn't matter—because I trust myself. That trust is then transferred to every person, place, or condition that I'm in. When I walk into a class filled with strangers for a training session, they don't know me. Yet a level of unspoken trust develops almost immediately between us.

It's all about how I show up. I show up being curious. I show up expecting to only see incredible people using their skills to transform themselves and become even better. I show up with what I call "the end in mind." I help them remove the blocks to achievement. All of a sudden they see I'm walking the walk. I'm always in integrity, and they see that. I'm not there to teach something that I don't do. I'm not there to "change" them; I'm there to help them transform the skills that they usually know but have stopped practicing. I just help them remember what they already know, and I show them the power of what they know.

When you walk the walk, talk the talk, and remain in integrity, you are transparent. There is no hidden agenda. There is no doubt that you are trustworthy.

That transparency comes from pure intent—to show up, to be present, to reflect back what trust feels like. When someone feels what trust is like, the word no longer holds any meaning. Trust just is.

KEY POINTS: TRANSFORM FEAR INTO TRUST

- Trust is authenticity combined with vulnerability.

- The more you trust yourself, the more you can trust others.

- Micro-managing often causes lack of trust because the employee thinks you expect a screw-up at any moment.

- Mastery of trust begins by looking at yourself, "What am I afraid of? Is it real or just my imagination?"

- When you walk the walk and talk the talk with no hidden agenda, there is no doubt that you are trustworthy.

Chapter 4

The Art of Awareness
Life in Five Short Chapters
By Portia Nelson

CHAPTER 1
I walk down the street. There's a deep hole in the sidewalk. I fall in. I am lost. I am helpless. It isn't my fault. It takes forever to find a way out.
CHAPTER 2
I walk down the same street. There is a deep hole in the sidewalk. I pretend I don't see it. I fall in again. I can't believe I am in the same place. But it isn't my fault. It takes a long time to get out.
CHAPTER 3
I walk down the same street and there is a deep hole in the sidewalk. I see it there, and still I fall in. It's a habit. But my eyes are open and I know where I am. It is my fault and I get out immediately.
CHAPTER 4
I walk down the same street. There is a deep hole in the sidewalk. I walk around it.
CHAPTER 5
I walk down a different street.

I learned not to be a victim of the world I see through the very same way the previous story was revealed—awareness and choices. Our conditioning and domestication from birth until now prepares us for situations that we will face with what we know. When faced with conditions or individuals that challenge us in new or different ways, we must learn that we can choose a response based on our conditioning or we can choose a new and different response based on newfound awareness of not doing the same things over and over again.

When I was a kid, we traveled a lot because my dad was in the Air Force. I remember being in Goose Bay, Labrador, when I was nine or ten. Seven of the family's eight children were born and living at home at that time. Coming from a large family, always competing for attention … it was crazy sometimes.

I spent a lot of time in nature. When I was in nature and I had no distracting stimuli, part of me felt so alive and so excited. There was no stress, there was just being present, and that was the only thing I did.

We settled in Noblesville, Indiana, when I was sixteen. I had grown up in a multi-cultural environment, but now the environment contained bigotry and hate. I began to question why things were the way they were, such hate and separation. But I realized that if I went out in nature, I had this ability to feel different, to feel alive. The silence, the wind blowing the leaves in the trees … that's it for me.

When I was 20, I started Tae Kwon Do. The training integrated mind, body, and soul, as it included meditation. In that space of silence, I got the same sensation of being totally alive and present as I always had while in nature. What started to drop away were my egocentric notions of being 20—of being cool, of being macho. People started approaching me and asking me, at 20, life questions. For the most part, I could respond with a question, and help them see things differently.

What was that openness about? I realize now that the conditioning of being quiet and still allowed me to be open and observant. In that observation the right and perfect question always came; I never had to think about it.

Dr. George Sheehan, author of *Personal Best* and *Going the Distance: One Man's Journey to the End of His Life*, said, "The mind's first step to self-awareness must be through the body." Part of becoming aware is becoming aware of your physical body. When you're stressed versus when you're relaxed. When you're mentally clear versus when all these thoughts from the river of unconsciousness are twisting around in your head. When that tension is there, you have emptiness inside. When that peace is there, you have wholeness inside. "Peace" sounds esoteric, but I refer back to that stillness. Taking a deep breath and becoming aware of your physical sensation causes stillness and allows peace to happen in that instant.

Sometimes people tell me that they have tried to concentrate on their breathing or meditate and are still distracted by the thoughts zooming around inside their head. "Jack, instead of feeling calm when I meditate, I'm exhausted." That's your conditioning from the river of unconsciousness. When you are attempting to breathe, you are introducing a new condition.

I'll talk later in the book about mastering conditions, but for now don't use the word "meditate." That implies doing something. I want you to just sit down, breathe, and put your awareness on your breath. If a thought comes in, return your awareness to your breath. Your awareness cannot be in two places at one time.

Here's a 54-second exercise you can try. Gently breathe in through the nose and exhale through the nose with the mouth closed. Gently, with no effort. Breathe in for a count of six, hold for four, and breathe out for eight. Breathe in … hold … breathe out. Breathe in … hold … breathe out. Breathe in … hold … breathe out. Just totally relax.

I'm willing to bet that you were focused on your breathing rather than your thoughts. I believe that wisdom speaks to us in the space between our thoughts.

This brings me to the spiritual aspect of mastering awareness. We seldom let the essence of who we are dance in the present moment. That part of us that is absolute truth, love, and acceptance seldom gets to show up.

Remember times when you felt a moment of peace? When you start having a moment of peace, and another moment of peace, and another, your experience is peace.

If you try to make yourself wrong for having thoughts instead of those moments of peace, all you have is judgment. It's OK to have those thoughts. When you have them, just put your awareness back on your body, back on your breathing.

Conditioning and the input that we have from TV, computers, or other outside sources are blocks to awareness. A friend of mine observed a class being taught to FBI agents. The instructor asked, "Who are you?"

"Well, I'm an FBI agent."

"But who are you?"

"I'm a great agent!"

"But who are you?"

After a lot of frustration and anger, it began to sink in: "Who am I? Wow." Most of the time we are conditioned to believe that what we do is who we are. That's truly not the case. That gets in the way of our awareness because what we do is not who we are.

Another block to our awareness is worry. Recently I heard worry described as a dynamic form of prayer. Your focus is on the worry, and it becomes so real that your heart, body, mind, and soul are so impacted, it impacts what you do. What if, instead of worrying, you prayed with that same intensity for what you really want? Something different might happen.

In a previous chapter I mentioned the "coulda, woulda, shoulda" self-talk that hooks us to the past. "Need to, want to, have to" hooks us into the future. If you've got one foot in the past and one foot in the future, you might very well miss what's going in the present moment.

A friend was once telling me about his brother-in-law, an auto worker in Michigan. Every time he visits, the brother-in-law says, "Man, one more day down, and I'm that much closer to retirement." After 20 years he's still doing this. He sees only what he doesn't have, which is the retirement. His conditioning, his orientation toward a future event, is contributing to him missing some very sacred moments from those 20 years.

Self-centeredness can play a big part in not being aware because we believe it's all about us. Most of the time we kid ourselves because we think something is about us—and it's not. This shows up a lot in victimhood. Victimhood is a state of mind where people can't see that the main thing still hurting them is their thoughts.

I was making a purchase in a home-repair store, and the clerk was having trouble with her computer. "I'm so stressed," she said.

I asked, "What are you stressed about?"

"Work," she said.

"What if it's not the work?" I asked. "What if it's the *thoughts* about the work?"

She looked at me. I could see in that instant that she had stopped to realize, "I have control over my thoughts."

How do you have control over your thoughts? One option is to slow the mind. You do that by breathing and being aware of your body, as I've already shown.

There are different levels of the mind, as shown by our brain waves. When we're totally awake and active, our brain waves operate at a state called beta where they oscillate between 14 to 30 cycles per second. When our minds relax and disconnect a bit from the world around us, our brain waves slow down too, oscillating between 8 and 13 cycles per second, which is the alpha state. We might be watching a movie or daydreaming in this state, which is a more internally focused awareness. Relaxing even more would put us in a theta state. The delta state is deep sleep.

My point is that alpha and theta states are more reflective and self-aware states. You want to train yourself to reach a theta state, where you are totally in the present, relaxed, aware, in that space. There is no thought required to get there.

Every time you can do that, you take that experience into what you do next. In situations where you used to be stressed, you show up differently, you react differently. People will ask, "Did you cut your hair?" "Did you lose weight?" They look at you differently because you show up differently.

You can master awareness with mental imagery because the brain doesn't know the difference between a real and an imagined experience. Studies have determined that when Olympic athletes run in certain events, certain muscles will fire. When they are sitting in a chair, imagining the event, the same muscles will fire. The brain is just an organ that collects information, stores it, and then brings it up when needed.

Let's say you have a condition at work that you don't like and you want to have a different experience. One way to have the possibility of a different outcome is to have people write out a paragraph or two about what they'd like to change in that condition.

Then I tell them to picture in their minds that the change has already occurred. I ask: "What do you feel like now that it has occurred?"

After they tell me, I ask: "What's the first thing that needs to change for you to get to that feeling?"

We break the condition down into observable behaviors that they can change, one by one, so they can get closer to that feeling. The key is to keep that mental image in their minds more often than not. That leads to the possibility of them seeing something different other than their problem.

I invited a leader to write out how he would like a meeting to go. He had great trepidation because this type of meeting never went well. After completing the exercise, he discovered that the meeting the next day unfolded almost exactly as his written description of how he would like for it to go. With that image written out and in your mind, you have the possibility of seeing that change occur.

It's the space between the thoughts where a new possibility shows up. Behavioral psychologists have determined we have about 65,000 thoughts per day, and many of those are from the day before, and many of those are from the day before that, and so on. If we always do what we've always done, change cannot occur.

That's why we need the space between the thoughts. How do we get there? Breathe. Use the technique I explained earlier: Breathe in for a count of six, hold for a count of four, and breathe out for a count of eight. That creates the space for a new possibility.

When that space is created, how much more powerful will that mental image be? How much more powerful will conversations be when you become the "conscious" creator of conversations before they happen? The possibility of no residue of doubt, mistrust, frustration, or stress might be present. You have a brand new canvas to paint on. Now what are you going to paint?

KEY POINTS: MASTERING AWARENESS

- Becoming quiet and still allows you to be open, observant, and able to summon forth the perfect question.

- Becoming aware of your breathing can bring you wholeness and peace, making you better able to consciously handle business situations.

- Instead of wasting time worrying, focus equally intensely on something you want.

- The mind's first step to self-awareness must be through the body.

- Concentrating on your breathing can allow change to occur in the space between your thoughts, thereby reducing stress and reenergizing your body and mind.

Chapter 5

Ask, Don't Tell

According to Hollywood lore, when filming the biblical epic The Greatest Story Ever Told, *director George Stevens wanted extra passion from John Wayne when delivering the highly significant line, "Truly, this was the Son of God."*

"You are talking about Jesus," Stevens told him. "You've got to say it with awe."

For the next take Wayne did just what he'd been told. He summoned his most intense feelings, paused dramatically, and said:

"Aw, truly, this was the Son of God."

What feelings are most intense with us as managers when we approach our employees? Do we pause even for an instant before we spew our emotional outburst and projections upon our employees? How can we become more conscious in leading others when we are not yet conscious of what we say and do?

We're at a period in time where leadership is not a position—it's a set of skills that are practiced over and over again that creates the possibility for change to happen.

Look at the history of many organizations. Many of those in leadership positions have no experience of being a leader; they were promoted simply because it's all about getting things done and they were good at getting things done. As a consequence, we define the people who work for us by what we know about *what we have done* rather than *what they know*. We don't develop leadership within that person. Instead, it's easier to tell them what to do.

Ironically, managers then get upset because the employees are not being proactive in their jobs. If you're always telling them what to do, you're conditioning them not to act until you say so. If you are proactive and always out front, an agent of change always asking questions of your employees, you will be full of expectations for everyone who works for you.

Now, sometimes it is appropriate to tell your employees what to do. Let's say your office building caught fire. You wouldn't go around to everyone asking, "Gee, what do you think we ought to do?" No, you'd tell them to call the fire department and get out of the building. Sometimes you have to respond to conditions and clients in the moment by giving instructions. It also depends on the level of knowledge with a task or procedure, as more telling will take place with a new procedure or task versus someone who has been in a position for a longer period of time.

To create awareness in your employees and help them see things differently, though, *your asking becomes a most powerful way to heighten an individual's awareness* rather than telling them what to do. "What do you think about this?" is a good way to wake your employee up, draw him or her out of the river of unconsciousness.

Let's say your employee responds "I don't know" to a question that you asked them. The response very well could be because of their conditioning. You might say, "I get the point that you don't know. But if you *did* know, what might be different?" That raises the possibility of them thinking about the issue and something happening differently.

If you train individuals to wait on you to tell them what to do, that's what will happen. If, instead, you ask masterful questions, those individuals are going to learn to ask themselves questions before they come back to you. It's quite possible that this will save you as a manager a huge amount of time. That's part of the conundrum of this style of leadership: As a leader, you're in essence teaching the employee to lead himself or herself.

Again, telling someone what to do is appropriate in some situations. You, as a leader, need to ask yourself: What is the conditioning that I'm displaying? Am I defining people by what I know? Do they know something that I don't, and would I learn it by asking questions? What am I missing by telling rather than asking?

I'm sure some managers will think: "I don't have time for a Q&A with every employee. I'm too busy! My calendar's chock-full! I can't waste time standing around asking people questions."

All right. Ask yourself: How much of that busy schedule is due to the fact that you have to keep telling people to fix things? Could it be possible that those things have to be fixed because the employee hasn't thought the situation through? What if asking masterful questions upfront could *save* you time in the long run?

One manager told me he spent 85 percent of his time in meetings. He laughed and said he spent 100 percent of the other 15 percent fixing problems. I asked, "What would it be like if you didn't have to spend all that time fixing problems because you asked the employee simple questions at the beginning?"

This idea isn't rocket science. What best serves the client? What best serves you? The telling is so ingrained and conditioned in many of us, but it's a short-term fix. The long-term fix is shifting your approach and asking masterful questions instead.

What are the benefits of asking? You get employee input that you wouldn't have otherwise. You get the benefit of the employee's creativity. You get the employee's buy-in that builds trust between you. And when you create trust, you create an environment where the possibility of change can occur. Productivity becomes higher. So does employee retention, because people are fully engaged in their jobs. Instead of going home at the end of eight hours burnt-out from the drudgery, your employees are now energized by their participation in the process. Asking creates benefits for your workplace and the client.

Think about some of the best conversations you've ever had. Often, it's because the other person listened instead of talked, and you felt you were fully heard. With the asking approach, it's up to you as a leader to create those moments where employees feel they are fully heard.

The change is in the image. Since the mind doesn't know the difference between what's real and what's imaginary, whatever image you have in your mind tends to occur. If you focus on problems, if you think an employee is lazy or stupid, that's all you're going to see. You can't see beyond that image. If you approach the situation with a curious mind open to all possibilities, then you have a possibility of seeing something different.

As a leader, your job is to guide the person to different, more empowering choices that they have not even considered—not because they are lazy, but because they were not consciously making the most powerful choice.

A good friend of mine came back all fired up from a workshop by self-help guru Tony Robbins. We were scheduled to have a coaching session, and I'm thinking, "What the heck can I teach this guy?"

I created a Nature's Retreat for him. This personalized program that I offer includes a three-hour walk in nature where I teach leaders to slow down and experience some space between their thoughts, a space where stress and tension is released.

So we went to a local park and proceeded to listen to the rhythms of nature. The gentle lapping of the water, the soft dancing of the wind in the trees ... We found ourselves slowing down, relaxing, and walking to those rhythms.

My friend said, "This walk has been a big change for me. I'm even breathing differently. For the first time in my life, I can feel my feet hitting the ground with each step. I feel like I'm really here now, and not thinking ahead or behind."

I had taken someone who had come from this huge, adrenalin-laced event into a foreign place where he'd never been before. And I'd done it just by asking questions and getting him to see himself in the "now" instead of in the "then."

My point is that if you consciously ask someone to think differently, he or she will go there. True, they might jump back into the river of unconsciousness as soon as you are through. But chances are that you only have to ask a masterful question to pull them out of the river of unconsciousness once again.

One of the Latin words that "educate" comes from is *educere*, which means "to lead forth." By asking masterful questions, you are leading forth, or pulling, incredible wisdom from your employees. Watching their faces, you can literally see that moment when they go from not thinking about the issue at hand to realizing that they are being invited to share their wisdom and experience and help arrive at a solution together. Wow! It's a powerful moment.

You say, "But what about the new worker, the one who just graduated from college or joined our business from another company? Since they're still learning what we do, won't they need to be told more than asked?"

Of course. But if you don't ask the new worker the masterful questions too, you miss gaining the valuable insight of someone who is not stuck in the river of unconsciousness. Because they are new to your business, you might gain a new perspective on your business or one of your practices that you had not considered before. All because you asked a question.

You can't *not* answer a question. Replies are automatic. You may not verbalize that reply at that moment, or even fully form your response, but it will stay in your head. I've had coaching sessions where I asked, "What's missing here? Think about it and let me know in two weeks." Sometimes I'm not really searching to find what's missing or even making the assumption that something's missing; instead, by asking the question, I'm drawing the person out of getting the same result over and over. They ask themselves what's missing and, in the process, come to consider the matter in a new way.

Here's a key point: You, as the asker, do not have to have the answers to every question. I do training all over the country, and I can't tell you how many times people have come up to me months or years later and said, "That question you asked us, that two or three minutes where I really started thinking, have changed my life."

Do you think I have a clue what that question is, what I said? No—but they do. It never left them.

Training used to be an event, but now I see it as an experience—a happening, as they used to say in the '70s. The ideal situation is that someone comes in and has an experience so powerful that it changes the way they think and do business. If that happens, they have the willingness to be truthful and to enroll the help of others around them to make those changes in their business. It's an interaction, a whole-body experience, where all levels have been touched.

At one class, several leaders talked about having to deliver personal development reviews that weren't positive to their employees. They had a lot of trepidation. I said, "Instead of telling the employee, why not ask them questions? Who, what, where, and how, but not why." In an uncomfortable situation, people tend to hear "why" as "Why did you do that, you idiot?"

All of them took the asking approach in their reviews. Even the poor reviews that had to be delivered became learning experiences rather than something charged with negativity.

KEY POINTS: ASK, DON'T TELL

- To create awareness and help your employees see things differently, ask, don't tell.

- Asking masterful questions causes employees to question themselves before coming to you. You are teaching them to lead themselves.

- If you consciously ask someone to think differently, he or she will do it.

- A person can't *not* answer a question; it automatically invites a reply.

- By asking masterful questions, you are pulling wisdom out of your employees.

- When someone says "I don't know," invite them with this gentle question, "But if you *did* know, what might be different?"

Chapter 6

Masterful Questions

This is a story about four people: Everybody, Somebody, Anybody, and Nobody.

There was an important job to be done and Everybody was asked to do it. Everybody was sure that Somebody would do it. Anybody could have done it, but Nobody did. Somebody got angry about that because it was Everybody's job. Everybody knew that Anybody could do it, but Nobody realized that Somebody wouldn't do it. And it ended up that Everybody blamed Somebody because Nobody did what Anybody could have done.

Sometimes, a simple question will alter the outcome of many situations where *everyone* assumes that *everybody* else is going to do what *somebody* was supposed to do and *nobody* did. The simplistic, yet powerful tool of any leader is asking a question that alters the thinking of the person being questioned.

A question in and of itself is an expression of inquiry that invites or calls for a reply. Note that it says "invites," not "demands." It's easy to interrogate, but you will get a different sort of response than one that is invited. You need to be aware of the type of questions that you're asking. The question "why" often keeps you stuck because you're talking about the cause of a past event that you can't change. You can't change the past; that's reality, and any time you argue with reality you lose and nothing changes.

Instead, questions should take this approach: "What needs to be different next time?" "Who needs to be informed when that is done?" Those are questions that keep moving space forward.

"Why" in itself is not bad, when asked in a state of curiosity. The problem is that it's usually asked in a state of interrogation: "Why did you make that mistake?" "Why didn't you do this the way I told you?" The wrong use of "why" is accusatory thinking. It communicates anger and frustration and creates mistrust. And you can't get positive results simply by reframing an accusatory question and not saying "why": "What were you thinking when you made that mistake?" That has the same implication.

You need masterful questions. When you are masterful at something, you are using skill and expertise. In this case, being expert is about simplicity. You keep going back to the simple questions: Who, what, where, when, how. They invite openness, invite the person to share. And in sharing, they invite the person to discover their greatness or reveal to themselves as to why something is working or not working.

The shorter the question, the better. Let's say you and I are talking about a situation. I ask, "What's missing?" Your brain goes to work and starts creating a visual image of what's missing. Then I ask, "What's the first thing that you need to do to change that?" Your brain creates that image too. It moves you to an observable behavior where I, as a manager and leader, can see you making a shift in your actions.

But you need to give the person time to answer your question before asking another. Often I see managers asking a question, then another, then another on top of that. That creates the mental equivalent of a three-car pile-up in your brain; nothing can move. The brain can only process one image at a time. If you're just piling on the questions, where's the clarity for your employee? You're just creating trouble for them.

Ask your question then shut up. Allow silence. In that silence is where the imagery is created and thinking starts. In that silence is the possibility of your employee doing something different than they have before. "Be still and know" is a powerful statement, because an image is being created in that stillness—an image that will help a person think differently than they've been conditioned. If you look at people who are creative, so often they will mention that creativity comes to them when they are quiet. Again, it's that space between thoughts that allows room for something new to happen.

I started out my working life at a steel foundry in Noblesville, Indiana, where I was a forklift operator. At 3000 degrees the steel and other materials were melted down into a liquid form of cast iron. That iron was poured into a ladle and transported by forklift to the next stage in the process. By the time the ladle of molten iron had reached its destination, a slag of impurities had formed on the top of the liquid metal; we had to pull off that slag before we poured the molten iron into the mold, and nine times out of ten it came out perfect.

Negative thinking is like that slag that must be removed before we have purity. We must be able to rake off what is not useful to us. Behavior psychologists have determined that approximately 77 percent of what you tell yourself is negative thinking; whatever you do will be 77 percent impure. That negative thought works against you. But if you ask questions, you are no longer in the river of unconscious thinking—you are in thought. That sounds cosmic, but all it means is that we are doing instead of thinking about it. We are riding the bike instead of *thinking* about riding the bike.

Nietzsche said that man thinks he thinks when in reality he is thought. That statement says to me that if we can get to the state of pure thought, we are 100 percent with whatever we're doing and we are totally present in the moment. If you're riding a bike, you're fully engaged in riding the bike and not thinking about something else—the groceries you must buy or the TV show you want to watch. If you are washing the dishes, you are fully and only washing the dishes.

It's a Zen approach to life, and there is even a name for this: Being present in the moment. Basically, any activity you think is mundane is not really if it is pure thought. Washing dishes, for example, becomes about awakening and being fully in the moment. When you are fully in the moment, you can see clearly and without judgment. You can fully appreciate what you are accomplishing, even if it is "only" washing the dishes.

Now let's apply living in the moment to the work we do as managers, as individuals. All too often, we as managers take for granted that our employees "work for us." What if it's not true? What if they're there for you to help them wake up? In that waking up, they will see something differently than they have before; experience something differently than they have before; and become engaged more than ever before. In that engagement, they become more productive. With that productivity, they help the company become more profitable.

What has to change for that engagement to take place? Let's say you try to fix a problem and conditions don't change in your workplace. Are the functions "messed up," or is the real problem that you as a manager are not helping people wake up?

Mastering questions is about finding the truth, and to find the truth you as a manager must invite your employees to speak their truth. You need to invite them to talk about the way they see things to find what's true. If four people saw a car wreck, there would be four different versions of what happened. Each observation would be different. Our responsibility as managers is to help our workforce discover what their truth is. In the process, you—and they—will discover why they do the things they do.

You must be conscious in this endeavor to keep your masterful questions short and succinct: Who, what, where, when, how, and never why. You must practice being quiet after asking a question. Masterful questions are a skill, and like any other skill you will need to do it over and over before you become good at it. Being masterful with questions is not always where the power lies; the most powerful moment is when you ask the question. It takes practice.

If this seems like unnecessary work, ask yourself: "What am I practicing now? Am I a master of frustration, or worry, or concern?" All I'm saying is become a master of questions.

A beginner mind is a good thing to have and keep, because you do not think you "know." Instead, you remain curious and engaged by whatever you are practicing or learning.

Here's an example: When I began my Tae Kwon Do school, I still practiced the basics, and I was always with the students wherever they were in the learning process. I was never above or below them, I never considered myself better or worse than they were. Being with them in that approach allowed me to stay in a beginner mind. Staying in a beginner mind allowed me to stay curious and continue learning. That's how I became a master of martial arts.

I am mastering coaching in the same way. My main practice as a coach is asking masterful questions. It's not about "knowing" how to coach. The minute I think I "know" anything, I am making an assumption—and you know what they say about those.

As a manager, you want to learn more about your employees. When you ask questions, you discover what happened and what needs to happen. Don't go into this with pre-supposed thoughts. Make your questions clear, with no assumptions and no agenda. Show up with a beginner mind, curious to learn, and the person you are talking to will respond honestly.

I always listen to what the person says and frame my question around their last few words of the last sentence they share. This makes my question relevant to where they are in their minds, their thought process. And when they answer the first question, you listen and then ask another question, again based on the last few words of the last sentence of the answer. That shows to the employee that you are listening to what he or she is saying, that you're in the moment with them and not judging or criticizing them.

All along you're paying attention to the person's body and how they're showing up in the moment. Are they frustrated or angry?

What about yourself? What are your face and body conveying? Is there an interrogative quality to your questions, or are you just showing up being curious? Keeping your questions neutral won't help if your facial expressions and body scream, "You screwed up!" In a state of fear and conditioning, an employee will give you the answer they think you want to hear, not the truth. That will dilute the purity of the answer. Is that what you want?

In Tae Kwon Do school, I would take brand-new students to the back of the class and have them practice kicking—let's say with the right leg, for the entire class. I would come back later and they'd be sweaty and exhausted and a little frustrated, but they'd demonstrate how they had learned to kick with the right leg. They were ready to move on to something besides kicking, but I'd say, "OK. Now let's practice the same movement with your *left* leg." And they'd work on it, not realizing that they were becoming ambidextrous and refining their kicking style as they practiced. A simple change of focus and another world of potential opened up.

There is often a misconceived notion that asking masterful questions is difficult to do. It's easy to do. It's just hard to put in place because all of us are sucked into the river of unconsciousness and go about our lives doing the same things over and over. Every time you ask a masterful question, it not only pulls your employee out of the current and puts them up on a rock where they can think. It puts *you* up there too. You're looking for something different from the other person. You make different choices yourself.

You will sink back into the river of unconsciousness from time to time, but as you keep asking questions you will become aware.

KEY POINTS: MASTERFUL QUESTIONS

- A masterful question is simple: who, what, where, when, how. It avoids "why" because that often sounds accusatory.

- Give the employee time to answer one masterful question before you ask another.

- To truly ask masterful questions, you must be 100 percent "in the moment," totally focused on the employee.

- Often being aware that you don't "know" something is good because it means you are still engaged and learning.

- Practice asking, and then staying silent.

Chapter 7

Verbal Imaging

Before the start of the 2006 football season, University of Florida head coach Urban Meyer gave each new freshman player a photograph of four Southeastern Conference championship rings and one national title ring. The photo represented what each player accomplished the last time the Gators won a national championship, in 1996. Meyer told his new players that this is what they were playing for and what they ultimately wanted to experience.

After their first loss, Meyer passed out a new card to each of his players. On one side was a photo of a national championship ring. On the other side was a quote from Danny Wuerffel, Heisman Trophy winning-quarterback on the Gators' 1996 national title team. That team had been down emotionally after losing to Florida State in the final regular season game. Wuerffel's quote said how the team bounced back from the loss to eventually win it all.

Continuing this process of visualization, University of Florida quarterback Chris Leak borrowed a national championship ring from a member of the 1996 team and wore it for a week to remind himself what the team was ultimately playing for.

In the championship game against Ohio State, Leak outplayed Ohio State quarterback Troy Smith, a recent Heisman Trophy winner. Leak completed almost 70 percent of his passes and passed for 212 yards, one touchdown, and no interceptions. The University of Florida beat Ohio State 41-14 to win the national championship.

One of the skills missing for many years from the world of training, coaching, and facilitating was the need for visualization. We were not aware that we think in images. As I've mentioned, if I say "garbage can," you don't think "g-a-r-b-a-g-e-c-a-n," your mind conjures up an image of a garbage can. Managers can harness this power by using masterful questions to create images in the minds of your employees.

When your mind creates a powerful image, you are in that image in that moment. This means there is no room for negative thoughts or contradictory images— only the image of what you want your employee to visualize.

Remember the example of athletes visualizing themselves executing the perfect dive or winning the marathon: The brain can't tell the difference between a real and an imagined experience. If you're really good at asking questions that plant an image in your employee's mind of what needs to get done in that moment, the thoughts they'll have, and the feelings too as they accomplish that task, then the possibility for change is much greater because they are having that experience of success or doing things different in that moment!. It's all about the power of verbal imaging. Verbal imaging helps to create a future reality in the moment and not some time or "what if" in the future.

Conversely, if most managers give a task to someone and they don't finish it successfully, the managers blame the employee rather than reflecting to themselves, "What did I not do or say, what did I not ask that person to help them make a commitment to get that job done?" I recommend you do this reflection and visualize yourself taking different steps in the encounter that would help the employee finish the job. In this instance you are using verbal imaging on yourself for a better outcome next time.

Verbal imaging will be more powerful if you utilize metaphors to paint pictures in other people's minds. A metaphor makes an idea clearer by comparing it to something else. Here's a familiar metaphor: "As nervous as a long-tailed cat in a room full of rocking chairs." Or: "There's no use crying over spilled milk." By planting a vivid image in the employee's mind, you help them become aware.

Recently I was watching a DVD at the house of a friend, a former employee of mine. He said, "Jack, something you told me years ago altered the way I live." I enquired as to what I said and he told me about a time when we were standing around at work one day talking. He was very upset about the situation we were discussing. I simply said, "Boy, you must really like drama," and walked away. He was so upset and angry at me.

But the image I had planted of him participating in his drama wouldn't go away, and he realized I was right. He shared that he has questioned himself ever since then if what he was dealing with was real or drama. That has helped him avoid a lot of unnecessary pain and stress in his life. That subtle image was so powerful that it altered the way he thought.

The best metaphors are short and succinct and make their point with laser-like accuracy. They create an anchor for a new way of thinking, and change, to begin. Anything that creates an image in the mind can be effective. As a manager, you need to help paint that picture, solidify that image. We know what needs to be done, and the metaphor helps the employee see what needs to be done.

There is always the risk the employee is not visualizing what you want him or her to. Just as they say no two snowflakes are exactly the same; no two people are the same. Each individual has a unique perspective shaped by the people, conditioning and events in his or her life.

Let's go back to the garbage can image. A child brought up in an exclusive high-rise apartment in Manhattan might visualize a tiny, shiny can with a designer label and a pedal to raise the lid, while a child brought up in Barrow, Alaska, might visualize a big, heavy, battered can that has to be kept under lock and key to discourage polar bears. If you use a metaphor to tell a group of 20 employees what to do, they will have 20 slightly different mental images of that task.

You address this issue through some simple questions. For example, you might ask one of the employees to explain what's expected. Then, using the last few words of his last sentence, you ask questions that help refine his mental image and clarify the task.

We're talking here about seeing the end. That's a critical piece of this approach. Most people are so focused on the problem, so focused on what's not working, that they get stuck and it's hard for them to see what the next step should be. If an employee is stuck in the moment, ask, "If everything was in place and you *were* successful in this task, what would you be doing? What would you be saying? What would your self-talk be?"

By seeing the end, you're really seeing the potential for greatness that already exists in each one of us. We just haven't tapped that greatness yet because we're too focused on "reality." Well, that same reality can include the task being completed. All we have to do is see the end, and if we do it masterfully enough our brain comes to accept it as reality. It's like taking a picture of the future.

Let me explain further. Let's say I have a digital camera and take a photo of you. It instantly shows you as you are, right here, and right in this moment. But if I took a photo of you with an old Polaroid camera, we would pull the film out of the camera and at first we'd see nothing. Then slight images would come into view. Then chemicals on the film would make the images become more and more solid and clear.

The process of seeing the end and seeing greatness is like taking that Polaroid shot. At first your visualization of the outcome will be blurry and indistinct. But the more that you solidify the image and focus on it, the more you increase the chances exponentially of that image becoming reality. In this case, the "chemicals" aiding the development of the image are the experiences you've already had. The "focus" is your awareness of the image that you want to create.

The basic image in a Polaroid shot would develop in a minute or so; the longer you allowed the photo to develop, the more all the other details would emerge. In the same way, the more time you devote to verbal imaging, the more solid the image of what you want to achieve becomes.

When I was teaching Tae Kwon Do, I would ask advanced students to break wood—two, three, four, five pieces together—and even concrete blocks with their fists. The key to success in this task is not brute strength, but the images they have in their minds. If they could break the wood or the concrete in their minds, then they could do it in "reality." If they thought the breaking wasn't going to happen, then it didn't happen. They couldn't break even a single piece of wood. That's the power of mental rehearsal and imagery.

When I'm coaching someone, I sometimes ask, "What would it be like if you had created a beautiful painting, it was hanging on the wall, and a stranger walked in and began smearing paint all over it?"

"I'd be upset!"

"All right then. What's the difference between someone smearing paint on that beautiful image you've created and you 'smearing paint' on an employee's mental image by always telling them what to do and not trusting in his own initiative?"

My point is that you need to have a blank canvas, so to speak, for every conversation with your employees, and then by asking masterful questions you help them paint their picture at that time, in that moment, in their mind as to what needs to change or happen. You have to come to the conversation in a state of curiosity, not a state of judgment or anger or frustration. Those all muddy up the canvas. You want them to paint the picture on a blank canvas so the image is crystal-clear.

What will the employee be doing, thinking, feeling when she succeeds at the task? All too often the image of failure is where people hang out. Managers are focused on what's not working. The more you focus on what's not working, that is what shows up.

To ensure success, plant an image of success. Acknowledge what the employee has done right and how that benefits the business and you personally. Each time she accomplishes a task, acknowledge it. Her attitude and actions will shift to an image of success because you're inviting her to see a different outcome.

Positive Psychology is the scientific study of the strengths and virtues that enable individuals and communities to thrive. According to its developer, Dr. Martin Seligman, positive psychology provides compelling evidence that individuals can increase their happiness by identifying and engaging in their signature strengths. The more we use these strengths, the more steadily we advance into the Good Life, a life of immersion, absorption, and flow.

By focusing only on the strengths and not the weaknesses of those around you, you can help guide them and develop their awareness. If you do that, you stop managing and start leading.

If you're still unsure how to distinguish between managing and leading, here's a simple test. Are you feeling frustrated, overly challenged, upset? You're managing. If you feel empowered, are seeing things differently, and are guiding others to accomplish what they couldn't before, you're leading.

Managing is struggling; leading comes from a higher position. That's a vista where you must go often. You get there through the acknowledgement of what's working with others.

The Beach Boys sang about "good vibrations," but that term can really mean a lot more than sun, sand, and surf. I recently watched a DVD that talked about how 99.99 percent of what we see is energy. Everything around us is made up of particles vibrating at different rates. The vibration rate determines what the particle will be.

In business terms the "particle" becomes what is in the moment. If you're focusing on what's not working, that becomes the physical reality. If you're totally upset about what someone has done, that shows up too as negative vibrations.

You need to get past all those filters about what's wrong and what the person did wrong and realize: It is what it is. Then let it go. Approach the conversation in a state of curiosity and ask masterful questions so the person can see a different outcome. It's OK to help the person see the consequences of different outcomes. The key is curiosity and approaching it with "good vibrations."

Can you maintain this curiosity all the time? Is there a way to be aware and enlightened all the time? Is it realistic? You will still likely slip into the river of unconsciousness, fall into old habits, and irritate people at times. I would ask again: What do you want to practice? What do you want people to remember from their conversations with you as a manager? Do you want them to leave frustrated or empowered?

If you practice anger and frustration, that will show up in all your encounters. But if you remember to practice curiosity, masterful questions, good vibrations, they will show up. The more you practice asking masterful questions, the more they show up in everything you do.

If we become conscious of what we practice, then others become conscious of it and are more likely themselves to have moments of awakening. They see the curiosity in you, they become more open to you, and the trust level is higher. If you are not getting along with your new hires, ask yourself: What is the trust level? What can I do to improve it?

How do you keep yourself from slipping back into the river of unconsciousness? Use the techniques we've discussed: Create a positive mental image of yourself being a successful leader. Practice seeing this mental image. You might put a colored Avery Label dot on your mirror or your computer as a simple reminder. Every time you see it, you remember to practice seeing your mental image of being a successful leader who asks masterful questions.

KEY POINTS: VERBAL IMAGING

- When your mind creates a powerful verbal image, you are in that image in that moment, with no room for negative thoughts or contradictory images.

- The metaphors in verbal images help employees see what needs to be done.

- A critical part of verbal imaging is seeing the end, the successful outcome, so our brain will accept it as reality.

- Every conversation with an employee should begin as a blank canvas, upon which they "paint" powerful images by asking masterful questions.

- Approach this canvas with curiosity and good vibrations instead of frustration or anger over the employee's past mistakes.

Chapter 8

Sacred Listening

In her ground-breaking book, The Art of Sacred Listening, *author Kay Lindahl writes, "The way we listen actually can allow another to bring forth what is true and alive to them"* ...

When it first happened to me, the person looked straight at me, like they weren't trying to balance their checkbook in their head at the same time. I had their full attention. They sat facing me, and they hung on every word.

Initially, it was very disconcerting. At that point I realized that I had not experienced this before, and I became aware that I felt special; it was an odd feeling that made me want to tear up. When I finished my thought, my new friend sat for a moment, then said, "What I hear you saying is that..." and reflected back to me my thought. Accurately.—Sally Santana, Workplace Spirituality

I once led a church service about sacred listening where one goes beyond communication skills, beyond active listening, to a place where all moments are sacred regardless of who you are with and where you are located. This moment, each moment, is sacred because you have reached a new level of awareness, one where each breath you take helps you to remember the sacredness of the silence and a new relationship is revealed to yourself and others.

Many came up to me after the service and revealed that they believe sacred listening needs to be brought to the business world. I could not agree more. What is missed when we are waiting our turn to talk? What is missed when what we have to say becomes more important than the person we are speaking to? When clients are with me, I give them my full attention because they are highly valued and important. I am totally present in the moment with what I call sacred listening.

Being present is rare in business because often a manager is thinking about the next thing. Those moments of full attention, of sacred listening, are needed to create the trust and engagement of your employees. The more moments of sacred listening that you have with them, the more engaged they will be in what you're asking them to do. This is called "heartfelt leadership."

In personal relationships we define intimate moments as ones in which we are completely connected and nothing else matters. But those moments are not limited to personal relationships. They can happen all the time at work or in a casual environment, such as chatting with a cashier at the hardware store. These are moments when you can awaken people and help them make a shift in their thinking. The more they shift, the more they feel the heart connection.

It's literally feel-good stuff. And if people start feeling good about coming to work, they feel good about serving whatever task you lay out for them. They start looking at it as more than a task; they are engaged in creating an inspiring environment.

Much of the focus of my life has been about spiritual awakening. Every job I've ever had has been about awaking the part of me that is not awake. Asking those questions led me to be more reverential about everything I do. When you come from a space of reverence, you don't internalize everything you hear, and you're very careful about what you verbalize. The more you connect with who you are, the more you realize that words matter and that they can create or destroy.

You make better choices, and since trust is the key to relationships, other people's willingness to awaken becomes much more viable than if you were constantly judging and criticizing them. Instead of being stifled by criticism, they are awakened by reverence. Start to listen differently and you will reflect on those times when you missed out because you were not indulging in sacred listening.

I took a leader who was really stuck in the river of unconsciousness to a large local park for a Nature's Retreat. He didn't know he repeatedly angered everyone around him. One of the first exercises I had him perform was to listen to the rippling of the water and the blowing of the wind through the trees, as well as study the reflections in the lake.

As a result of being immersed in a totally different environment, he was listening differently, doing more internal listening. He realized that people were not trying to do things to him, that he had been the one who was not listening to what needed to be said and done. In that moment, he realized he had danced more in the past, in what *had* happened, rather than being totally present and listening to the person he's with, listening to what needs to be done.

Sometimes we doubt what we hear when we listen, mainly because we doubt what we hear when we listen to ourselves. Our inner wisdom speaks to us in the space between our thoughts. We seldom calm our thoughts down enough to hear anything. When we hear something different that pulls us out of the river of unconsciousness, we don't take action. We continue to get messages, "This is what I need to do," and we still don't listen. That's because we doubt our abilities. If we practice doubt, doubt shows up. What you practice must be constant for there to be real change.

When I coach someone, whether in business or the martial arts, I choose a practice and I am constantly in the moment with them. I'm confident about what I hear in the space between my thoughts, and am more present and clear in asking questions that help awaken the other individual to what they know.

I once began a program in spirituality, using a text with many theories and stories. I soon became frustrated. I was on the verge of throwing the book away because the text was too obscure and complex for my ego. Instead, I started to ignore my frustration with the text, simply read it without judgment, and practiced the daily lessons.

After a while, I realized I was earning the equivalent of a black belt in spirituality. At the end of three years, when I joined a group based on this program, the text made perfect sense to me because I had been practicing the daily lessons instead of trying to figure them out.

Our minds constantly filter information and thoughts based on cultural, gender, generational, and religious factors—everything from our background is a type of filter. These show up in every conversation we have. We need to be more cognizant of those filters and the judgments we make based on them. That helps us become present in the moment. We can realize, "Hey, that's not my current agenda. That's one of my filters talking." If you're unconscious to them, they will definitely show up, and you'll spend more time being in judgment and upset than being awake and listening.

The best practice is just to ask questions. When you are asking questions, you seldom will make assumptions. It's very hard to make judgments because you're in a curious state of truly wanting to know. As the other person answers, you practice sacred listening and being in the moment with them. That way you really hear what he or she is saying.

In one of the exercises in a program I teach, I pair everyone off and have them sit back to back. Each person talks for two minutes about his or her passion in life. For two minutes, the individual releases everything he or she has ever dreamed of doing. Then, in seven words or less, the other person has to tell the essence of what was said relating to body, mind, and soul. The person who listened has to listen totally differently than you usually do.

As a result of this powerful exercise, you realize someone heard you and helped you discover what needs to be done.

Ultimately sacred listening is about empathy. An absolute knowing that is not explainable shows up, where I can hear the other person and know instantly what behaviors they need to change.

The practice that has brought me to this point is simply focusing on my breath. Some people may call it meditation, but I think of it simply as breathing practice. During those times of practice, there is no thought. When I practice breathing with another person, that space contains an invitation for the other person to speak and share their challenges and problems. They see the safeness in that sacred listening. It's no longer a regular conversation. Even in a store, with a salesman angry or upset about something, if you breathe and provide that silence in which they may speak, they will share.

The highest form of listening is empathetic listening. And you develop that skill when you are more aware of *how* you listen. When you're in a state of empathetic listening, you pay more attention to the words, the tone people are using, the position of their bodies. You have a heightened awareness of the content and context based on your awareness of everything that is said and not said. If you go into a discussion with an employee with empathetic listening, all the conditioning and barriers between you are reduced greatly.

This is hard for managers because you are conditioned to speak, to take charge, to give instructions or orders. Just remember this: I don't know anyone who has *listened* their way out of a relationship. I know plenty of people who have talked their way out of one.

KEY POINTS: SACRED LISTENING

- Sacred listening involves being totally present in the moment.

- The more you connect with who you are, the more you realize that words matter and that they can create or destroy.

- Being cognizant of the filters of our backgrounds and experiences, as well as the judgments we make based on them, will help keep us awake and listening instead of upset and critical.

- When you're in a state of empathetic listening, you pay more attention to people's words, tone, body language, and the context of everything said.

- No one has ever listened their way out of a relationship. Plenty of people have talked their way out of one.

Chapter 9

The Art of Choices

Mohandas [Mahatma] Karamchand Gandhi, the great Indian statesman and spiritual leader, was boarding a train one day with a number of followers. One of his shoes fell off his foot into the gap between the train and platform, where he could not get it. He promptly took off his other shoe and threw it down by the first.

Noting his fellow travelers' puzzlement, Gandhi explained that a poor person who finds a single shoe is no better off. What's really helpful is finding a pair.

Most of the choices we make are choices we have learned over our lives because of our past conditioning. When we become aware, we realize we can practice the art of choices. No longer do we have to take our past thoughts as the gospel, or accept all the conditioning we have received from our parents or others. We realize, "Hey, I can make choices, and I'm responsible for them."

When you are in management, you have to choose differently. Most of the time choices have to be made in the moment. In that moment, your choice becomes your practice. Whatever you practice shows up in that choice on the spot.

What is a "good" choice? That's a relative term. Any choice that creates trust would ultimately be a good choice. A good choice is one that creates choice for your employee, whether he or she will continue to drift along in the river of unconsciousness doing the same old thing or whether he or she will shift her behavior.

As a manager, you need to think before you say anything or ask masterful questions. The choices you give your employees must allow them to make the decisions. You can't tell them what to do. They must discover the consequences and what they need to do. Through the choices you give them, you help them uncover a new way of doing things differently. You're always in that place of helping them uncover their choices instead of directing them to change.

Sacred listening and intuition play a big part in this. You must know yourself and the space between your thoughts where you can listen differently. Intuition plus that ability to listen allows you to intuit what's going to happen next, or be said next, or what actions will be taken next. In regards to managing the contextual part, you can observe the body, words, and tone and know something that needs to be said or done. There's nothing mystical about it. You are able to intuit what needs to be said and what needs to be asked in this exchange with the employee.

The first ingredient of the art of choices is being aware. Without awareness, there is no choice except the unconscious one. Without being aware, as a manager, you always see what you always saw. Nothing will change until you realize that this person, place, or condition is not out to screw up your life. Until you become aware, you will always see that person, place, or condition as a problem or a challenge. The moment you become conscious, you ask yourself: "How can I see this person, place, or condition differently?"

The second ingredient of the art of choices is the power of questions. You need to ask the question differently than the problem, or you will be stuck. Einstein said, "We can't solve problems by using the same kind of thinking we used when we created them." In other words, if you always view the problem from the same unconscious level, you will always get the same result over and over.

The third ingredient of the art of choices is just to be the observer. When you observe the response, observe the changes. That way, you ask your next question based on what you've observed rather than being caught in the river of unconsciousness.

Someone once said that 98 percent of our thoughts are from the day before, and 98 percent of those thoughts are from the day before that, and so on. That's why we have beliefs and behaviors. In that unconscious realm of choices, we go through daily life doing what we always knew. When we become conscious, everything shifts. We start playing at a different level. You must always ask conscious questions to make conscious choices. The more awake you are, the better your choices will be.

"Critical thinking" is one of those buzzwords overused in our society, but it's no more and no less than the ability to make a conscious choice. All the courses and all the procedures about critical thinking simply come down to the ability to make a conscious choice. And when you are conscious of yourself, the more you can ask of others.

Self-awareness plays a huge role in critical thinking. One of my clients was willing to take a hard look at his conditioning and what he thought he was seeing in a relationship. He said, "I'm really embarrassed to admit this, but it's not about the other person at all. It's all self-centered." In that moment of self-awareness, everything changed in that relationship. He awoke to consciously play in the relationship and was able to create new choices.

Self-management is another aspect of critical thinking. We start to accelerate what we want to create in our work environment, our relationships, the immediate people around us, and everyone we interact with.

There are only two kinds of choices—unconscious and conscious. When you are in the midst of a critical business decision or a heated argument, most choices are made at the unconscious level. If you take a look at the unconscious choices you've made in your life, you'll discover that they eventually caused feelings of victimhood, anger, or blame. Then one day you wake up and realize that things don't bother you so much. You realize that people are not out to get you or attack you. You start making conscious choices.

How conscious are you at making choices in the moment? There are four levels of learning:

- **The unconscious incompetent.** You don't know what you don't know, so you can't do much about making different choices. Remember Alfred E. Newman from the old *MAD Magazine*: "What, me worry?" You're like that, ignorant of other possibilities.

- **The conscious incompetent.** Now you're aware that you can make different choices, and have a new level of awareness about choices. But all too often you slip right back into your old unconscious behaviors. I'd compare it to driving down a long empty stretch of highway and suddenly you see another car approaching from the other direction. Your attention is fixated on this new thing that has come into your awareness and you're observing its every detail. Suddenly one of your favorite songs comes on the radio and just like that, you're singing along and forget about the other car.

- **The conscious competent.** Here you've practiced the art of choices long enough that things aren't new anymore. You're good at being in the moment ... but you have to *think* about being in the moment before you're there. I'd compare it to a golfer who has to think about his new stance before he assumes it at the tee.

- **The unconscious competent.** This is the ideal state when it comes to practicing the art of choices. You don't have to think about it. You just practice. You're like a teenage diver who has visualized each step in her dive over and over and practiced the dive over and over until she gets to the Olympics and does it perfectly without thinking. It's second nature.

Change is incredibly simple. It's a matter of asking conscious questions so you can practice the art of choices. I recently had a client who was stressed out. I had him take a pen and a piece of paper, and I said, "Finish this sentence: 'Change is ...'"

He wrote: "Change is difficult."

"You're right—it is," I said. "Now finish this sentence: 'Change is …'"

He gave me a weird look, but he wrote, "Change is frustrating."

"Boy, is it ever," I said. "Now finish this sentence: 'Change is …'"

And that's how it went: "Change is constant." "Change is always happening." By the sixth or seventh time, he couldn't think of anything else. He just stared at the piece of paper with the words: "Change is."

"Yup," I said. "Change is. That's our lesson for today."

His body seemed to melt, the stress literally faded away. He had never thought about change simply in that context: "Change is." His first response, "Change is difficult," came from where his belief system is now and the fact that he's stuck there with a lot of frustration and angst in his body. What's the one thing he can practice to make a different choice about that situation? A simple chant: "Change is."

If you're conscious and making choices, you don't have to worry about the results. That doesn't mean you won't. That doesn't mean you won't be resistant to change. We human beings are masterful at complicating our lives. The old paradigm is "It can't be that simple," but what if it is? The real problem is that we're reacting to it as unconscious competents. You need to practice the art of choices until it's second nature, just like that Olympic diver. Let me repeat: It's all about what you practice.

Another client of mine was frustrated at everything going on in her life. She went on and on describing all the bad things that were happening. Finally I simply made the statement: "So you've decided to be a master at frustration?"

She looked at me and then started laughing. "I have, haven't I?"

"Yeah, you have," I said. "That's because you've been practicing frustration."

She had gotten so good at frustration that frustration was all she saw. But from that moment of self-awareness, she started to see things differently and to make different choices.

When you deal with your employees as a manager, your masterful questions are key to helping them practice the art of choices. Just as I did with her, you can bring them up three levels, from an unconscious incompetent to a conscious competent, just by asking a masterful question.

That doesn't mean they won't fall back into the river of unconsciousness. They will. That's their conditioning. But then you ask another masterful question to wake them up, and then another, and then another.

KEY POINTS: THE ART OF CHOICES

- The choices you give your employees must allow them to make the decisions. You cannot tell them what to do.

- Without awareness, the only choice is the unconscious one.

- You need to ask the question differently than the problem, or you will be stuck.

- When you observe the response or the change, you ask your next question based on what you have observed rather than slipping back into the river of unconsciousness.

- The ideal state for the art of choices is the conscious competent who practices it without thought.

Chapter 10

The Art of Practice

One day the Buddha was teaching a group of people. One man was upset and very vocal about it.

The Buddha listened patiently as the man vented his anger, and then he asked the group, "If someone gives a gift to another person, who then chooses to decline it, tell me, who would then own the gift? The giver, or the person who refuses to accept the gift?"

"The giver," said the group after a little thought.

"Any fool can see that," sneered the angry stranger.

"Then it follows, does it not, that whenever a person tries to abuse us, or to unload their anger on us, we can each choose to decline or to accept the abuse; whether to make it ours or not," the Buddha said. "By our personal response to the abuse from another, we can choose who owns and keeps the bad feelings."

My most practical advice to you is to ask: What's your practice? What will be your commitment to keep? Allowing people to practice the art of choice is a shift, a different experience than anything you usually do in the workplace. The profundity of the experience changes people—not managers asking questions. Instead of profundity, that's redundancy.

Think about it. If your boss says the same thing to you over and over, he is doing a masterful job of conditioning you not to listen. All too often people in organizations rise to positions of leadership because they're good at getting things done, but few have had training as leaders or managers. Their frustration arises when the people who used to work with them don't get things done. The more the manager points out the problem, the more likely the employees are to continue stuck in that place, and the more the manager continues trying to "fix" them. It's a vicious cycle.

I was leading an all-day class where all the managers were complaining, "I'm so exhausted. I constantly have to tell my employees what to do. I constantly have to fix this or that at work."

Finally I said, "Nobody needs fixing."

All the top leaders looked at me.

"They don't need fixed because nobody's broken," I said. "It's just the way they're conditioned. By fixing things yourself and by telling them what to do, you're the one conditioning them to fail."

I could see it was making sense with them, so I continued, "Your responsibility is to wake them up. You're the ones who are not helping them wake up."

Wow. They would have loved to fire me if it wasn't true. If they hadn't paid for the class, they probably would have walked out. Fortunately, at the end of the class, the head person said, "That was the one of the most enlightening classes I've ever attended."

When you are dancing in truth, you are not a threat. When you are dancing in an illusion of truth, you are a threat. Whatever we practice always shows up.

You want to practice being conscious. To help my clients wake up, I always tell them that when they're in a meeting that hasn't gone well, their thinking is getting in the way of practicing the art of choices. "Your thinking is stinking," I tell them and recommend that instead of thinking or talking, they take a deep breath. In that space of breathing, between thoughts, you create the space for a new, better thought to occur. You center yourself, and from that centeredness everything can evolve. When you are acting and reacting from a fear-based perspective, nothing can evolve.

An example is my martial arts conditioning; I could show up in an engineer's office in the auto industry in Michigan to talk about his product, without knowing anything about the product. I had trained myself to be calm and centered and ask great questions and be involved in what the guy was saying. I was able to build a trust level and could say, "What other questions might you have?" Then we would converse about his needs. If I did not have the answers to share with him, then I said I would get back to him once I had consulted the experts. I was seldom nervous in those meetings. I would concentrate on my breath and hear what he was saying.

We often use the term "brainstorming" to describe creative thinking, but the negative form of that is "mindstorming." Seventy-five percent of the time our thoughts are working against us. This huge storm of thoughts seldom has anything to do with the present or what you're about to do. Instead, you have fear-based thoughts, doubts about your ability, and judgments about the person, place, or condition in front of you. You're getting all worked up, all frustrated, and nothing useful is showing up.

To move out of the space, ask yourself, "What am I practicing? I'm practicing frustration. Where is the frustration coming from? Well, it's about ..." This helps you come up with the truth about where you are in your evolution to a conscious being.

I recommend you come up with a simple statement that has meaning to you to help center yourself, just as "Change is" helps my stressed-out client center himself. That statement will be different for each person; I can't tell you what it is for you. Because none of us are alike, the answers will always be different even if the question is the same.

Ultimately, whatever you practice has to be simple. In martial arts there are seven basic moves you must master before you can become a black belt. You practice those seven simple moves over and over, hundreds, even thousands, of times. Each time your awareness and practice of those moves becomes higher and higher until eventually you can see something and it's done. You want to break a board, it's done. Someone rushes at you and there is no thought of defending yourself. You simply do what needs to be done.

The same is true of practicing asking masterful questions. You don't worry about the result. The simplicity of the masterful questions will awaken the other person and create a shift in behavior and different results.

Always see your practice. By that, I mean be clear with yourself about what you really want and give yourself time to practice. Let's say you're stressed because change happens all the time in your workplace. Ask yourself: "What would I be like if I wasn't stressed? Would I be more approachable or standoff-ish? What would that moment of not being stressed look, feel, sound like?" If you're not clear about what needs to be done, this exercise helps you realize what you need to do in your practice.

Many of us worry, "But how will I do this? How will I do that?" The reality is that you can stew and get stressed about doing the next thing … or you can simply *do* it.

And don't "try" anything. "I'll try to remember"—well, will you or won't you? "Try" is the wimpiest of words. It delays or puts off acting. Jedi Master Yoda in the Star Wars movies told his student "Do or do not… there is no try." He's absolutely right. It's hard to be frustrated when you're active. Instead of letting negative thoughts seep in, simply do it and say, "Next!"

Do it now. Be here now. You will accomplish so much. If you honor this moment, then whatever you do in the next moment will be sacred as well because you'll be totally in that moment when it comes. Don't prostitute the moment to your worries and concerns.

The more you practice, the more results you will see. One of my clients is practicing seeing people in a different way—as they are, in each moment, rather than as he projects them to be with the baggage of past encounters. As a result, all those relationships are changing because he is honoring the moment in each encounter.

Practice makes permanent. I left active martial arts discipline in 1984, and my body will still do what I trained it to do 25 years ago. It's part of who I am. What you practice will lead to a permanent state of being. In the moment you can choose what is best for you and everyone.

I used to drive the people I worked with crazy. Whenever they came up to me with a story about whatever happened, I'd say, "Perfect."

"Jack, I lost one of our old accounts."

"You did? Perfect."

"Jack, our sales are down 10 percent."

"Perfect."

They'd get frustrated and say, "Aren't you hearing what I'm saying? How can you say that's perfect?"

I'd just look at them and say, "It happened in the past. Can you change the past? No? It's perfect."

That was my way of saying "Next!" When you make choices from a place of centeredness, you cannot be a victim. You can choose to practice choices. "Perfect" and "Next!" were the simple phrases that helped center me.

All practice is physical. Even if you're doing mental imagery, you must be in a physical state of being, cognizant of your body, your breathing. You want to train your body so that you are not in a state of "becoming" relaxed—you're simply there. Train the physical until the images in your mind are so powerful that you're instantly there. At the minimum, breathe. Leave the activity of your mind and concentrate on your breathing.

Always be cognizant of the physical practice you're in. Then your mind becomes full of what you want to create as opposed to what you fear.

That's the level I want you to aim toward. I want you to instantly realize the energizing and inspiring concepts I've described in this book because that is what you practice. It's always at the forefront of your mind. You may go about your day being an accountant, a steelworker, a lawyer, but you always show up making conscious choices. You each show up differently because your practice is different.

Here's the final piece of the puzzle. If the image of what you want to create is always in your mind, eventually you become that image on a physical, mental, emotional, even a molecular level. So here's the question to ask yourself "How can I practice what I want to see and what I want to be?"

KEY POINTS: THE ART OF PRACTICE

- Practice being conscious.

- Come up with a simple statement to center yourself when your brain is running wild.

- Whatever you practice, keep it simple.

- Instead of worrying about doing the next thing, just do it.

- Always keep the image of what you want to create in your mind. Eventually you will become that on all levels.

- Practice what you want to see and what you want to be.

Skills Practice

- Be aware of your breathing for thirty days, and you will calm yourself and lower your blood pressure and stress. Practice breathing in through your nose for the count of six, hold for four, and breathe out for eight. Practice this breath three times every hour on the hour.

- In changing behavior, view and change the deed and do not judge the do-er.

- Masterful questions can help an employee uncover and discover what has already worked and solidify the image of those practices in his or her mind.

- Reflecting on what needs to change in you is like throwing a pebble into a still lake reflecting the landscape around it. Only then can you distinguish between reality and illusion and become clear about what needs to be done to establish trust.

- Because the brain doesn't know the difference between real and imagined imagery, you can master awareness with mental imagery.

- As the asker, you are not required to have the answer to every question—merely an open, curious mind and a genuine interest in helping your employees succeed.

- When you ask masterful questions, listen carefully to the employee and frame your question around their last few words in each reply.

- If an employee is stuck in the moment, ask, "If everything was in place and you were successful in this task, what would you be doing? What would you be saying? What would your self-talk be?"

- If you are concentrating on your breathing, you cannot have room for thought. Concentrating on your breathing can help you listen to another person without judgment.

- Ask the employee to complete the thought "Change is ..."

About Jack Needham
Executive Coach, Motivational Speaker, Master Trainer

Whether in individual coaching sessions or leadership development classes, Jack Needham leads people to identify self-defeating behaviors and helps them make powerful choices to achieve their goals. With his perceptive insights into human nature and his ability to relate to people on spiritual and emotional levels, Jack inspires individuals and organizations to change and grow by asking masterful questions and holding them accountable for their actions.

Jack has been training and coaching individuals in the art of self-awareness and personal growth for more than twenty-five years. His specialty is leadership development and executive coaching. He is proficient in assessing needs, formulating solid action plans, influencing effective solutions, designing and implementing complete training programs, and building effective teams.

Jack, an ordained minister and a published author, holds a second-degree black belt in Tae Kwon Do and a BS in education. He is a member of American Society of Training and Development (ASTD) and the International Association of Coaches (IAC).

As a master certified trainer for The Coaching Clinic©, Jack brings his unique talents, skills, and abilities to a widely diverse audience of organizations locally, nationally, and internationally. As a certified Life Coach© and Self-Talk© trainer, Jack utilizes his motivational psychology skills to guide individuals in finding inspiration, creativity, and energy inside themselves. The result: they live the life they were truly meant to live.

For more information visit
www.stopfixingstartleading.com
or e-mail Jack at jack@stopfixingstartleading.com

Printed in the United States
220211BV00001B/5/P